DATE DUE			

796.7
DOE

Doeden, Matt.

Motocross freestyle

Lexile: 710

Woodland High School
Henry County Public Schools

To the Extreme

Motocross Freestyle

by Matt Doeden

Reading Consultant:
Barbara J. Fox
Reading Specialist
North Carolina State University

Capstone
press

Mankato, Minnesota

Blazers is published by Capstone Press,
151 Good Counsel Drive, P.O. Box 669, Mankato, Minnesota 56002.
www.capstonepress.com

Library of Congress Cataloging-in-Publication Data
Doeden, Matt.
    Motocross freestyle / by Matt Doeden.
    p. cm.—(Blazers. To the extreme)
    Includes bibliographical references and index.
    ISBN 0-7368-2729-3 (hardcover)
    ISBN 0-7368-5225-5 (paperback)
    1. Motocross—Juvenile literature. 2. Extreme sports—Juvenile
literature. [1. Motocross. 2. Motorcycle racing. 3. Extreme sports.] I. Title.
II. Series: Doeden, Matt. Blazers. To the extreme.
GV1060.12.D64 2005
796.7'56—dc22   2003026626

Summary: Describes the sport of motocross freestyle, including tricks
    and safety information.

Editorial Credits
Angela Kaelberer, editor; Jason Knudson, designer; Jo Miller,
    photo researcher; Eric Kudalis, product planning editor

Photo Credits
Artemis Images/Indianapolis Motor Speedway, cover
Corbis/Luca Babini, 26; NewSport/Larry Kasperek, 13, 25
David's Photography/William Crane, 15
Getty Images/Elsa, 5, 6, 7, 8, 19, 28–29
Kinney Jones Photography, 11
SportsChrome, Inc., 16–17, 21
Steve Bruhn, 12, 14, 20
X-Gen Photo/Anthony Scavo, 22

Table of Contents

Heavy Metal

A motocross rider revs his engine.
He speeds over a ramp into the air.
The rider kicks up his legs as he
grabs the handlebars and seat.

The rider stretches his legs behind the bike. He lets go of the handlebars and seat. The rider is not touching any part of the bike.

The rider grabs the seat and jumps back on the bike. The bike lands hard on the ramp. The rider gets ready to do his next trick.

BLAZER FACT

The X Games is a famous extreme sports competition. Only the top freestyle riders compete in the X Games.

Freestyle Bikes

Freestyle motocross began when riders did tricks during races. Some riders liked doing tricks better than racing.

Freestyle bikes have sturdy frames and strong suspension systems. These parts help the bikes take hard landings and crashes.

Freestyle bikes have knobby tires.
The tires grip the ramps and dirt
hills on the freestyle courses.

Handlebars

Fender

Seat

Knobby tire

Tricks

Grabs are popular tricks. Riders let go of the handlebars. They grab another part of the bike with one or both hands.

The rock solid is a daring trick.
The rider stretches out over the bike
and lets go.

During other tricks, riders stretch over the handlebars. Sometimes the bike is almost straight up in the air.

BLAZER FACT

In 1999, 15-year-old rider Travis Pastrana won the first gold medal in freestyle motocross at the X Games.

safety

Equipment helps keep riders
safe. Riders wear helmets, gloves,
and boots. Some riders wear
body armor.

Riders should never try dangerous tricks alone. Practicing with a friend helps freestyle riders safely enjoy their sport.

BLAZER FACT

Freestyle motocross is the only sport included in both the Summer and Winter X Games.

One-handed Superman seat grab

Glossary

body armor (BOD-ee AR-mur)—a plastic shield with foam lining that motocross riders usually wear under their clothing

frame (FRAYM)—the body of a motocross bike

freestyle (FREE-stile)—a type of motocross riding that focuses on tricks, stunts, and jumps

rev (REV)—to increase an engine's speed

suspension system (suh-SPEN-shun SISS-tuhm)—a group of springs and shock absorbers that helps soften the impact of landings on motocross bikes

Read More

Blomquist, Christopher. *Motocross in the X Games.*
A Kid's Guide to the X Games. New York: PowerKids
Press, 2003.

Schaefer, A. R. *Extreme Freestyle Motocross Moves.*
Behind the Moves. Mankato, Minn.: Capstone
Press, 2003.

Schwartz, Tina P. *Motocross Freestyle.* Dirt Bikes.
Mankato, Minn.: Edge Books, 2004.

Internet Sites

FactHound offers a safe, fun way to
find Internet sites related to this
book. All of the sites on FactHound
have been researched by our staff.

Here's how:

1. Visit *www.facthound.com*
2. Type in this special code **0736827293**
   for age-appropriate sites. Or enter a
   search word related to this book for a
   more general search.
3. Click on the **Fetch It** button.

FactHound will fetch the best sites for you!

Index